Bond

Maths
Assessment Papers

12+–13+ years

David Clemson

Nelson Thornes

Published in 2011 by:
Nelson Thornes Ltd
Delta Place
27 Bath Road
CHELTENHAM
GL53 7TH
United Kingdom

13 / 10 9 8 7 6 5 4 3

A catalogue record for this book is available from the British Library

ISBN 978 1 4085 1718 5

Page make-up by Tech Set Ltd

Printed in China by 1010 Printing International Ltd

Before you get started

What is Bond?

This book is part of the Bond Assessment Papers series for maths, which provides **thorough and continuous practice of all the key maths content** from ages five to thirteen. Bond's maths resources are ideal preparation for SATs exams, preparation for the 11+ and higher selective school entrance exams.

What does this book cover and how can it be used to prepare for exams?

Maths 12+-13+ is intended as practice for 12+ and 13+ exams. The coverage is matched to the National Curriculum, so will also provide invaluable preparation in the run up to Key Stage 3 SATs. It can also be used for very advanced practice for selective exams at 11. One of the key features of Bond Assessment Papers is that each one practises **a wide variety of skills and question types** so that children are always challenged to think – and don't get bored repeating the same question type again and again. We believe that variety is the key to effective learning. It helps children 'think on their feet' and cope with the unexpected.

What does the book contain?

- **20 papers** – each one contains 50 questions.
- **Tutorial links throughout** – B 5 – this icon appears in the margin next to the questions. It indicates links to the relevant section in *How to do ... 11+ Maths*. Our invaluable subject guide that offers explanations and practice for all core question types that are commonly found on 11+, 12+ and 13+ exam papers.
- **Scoring devices** – there are score boxes in the margins and a Progress Chart on page 60. The chart is a visual and motivating way for children to see how they are doing. It also turns the score into a percentage that can help decide what to do next.
- **Next Steps Planner** – advice on what to do after finishing the papers can be found on the inside back cover.
- **Answers** – located in an easily-removed central pull-out section.

How can you use this book?

One of the great strengths of Bond Assessment Papers is their flexibility. They can be used at home, in school and by tutors to:

- set **timed formal practice tests** – allow about 30 minutes per paper in line with standard entrance exam demands. Reduce the suggested time limit by five minutes to practise working at speed.

- provide **bite-sized chunks** for regular practice.
- **highlight strengths and weaknesses** in the core skills.
- identify **individual needs**.
- set **homework**.

It is best to start at the beginning and work through the papers in order. Calculators should not be used.

Remind children to check whether each answer needs a unit of measurement before they start a test. If units of measurement are not included in answers that require them, they will lose marks for those questions. To ensure that children can practise including them in their answers, units of measurement have been omitted after the answer rules for some questions.

If you are using the book as part of a careful run-in to an exam, we suggest that you also have another essential Bond resource close at hand:

How to do … 11+ Maths: the subject guide that explains the key question types practised in selective entrance exams. Use the cross-reference icons to find the relevant sections.

See the inside front cover for more details of this book.

What does a score mean and how can it be improved?

It is unfortunately impossible to guarantee that a child will pass a 12+ or 13+ exam if they achieve a certain score on any practice book or paper. Success on the day depends on a host of factors, including the scores of the other children sitting the test. However, we can give some guidance on what a score indicates and how to improve it.

If children colour in the Progress Chart on page 60, this will give an idea of present performance in percentage terms. The Next Steps Planner inside the back cover will help you to decide what to do next to help a child progress. It is always valuable to go over wrong answers with children. If they are having trouble with a particular question type, follow the tutorial links to *How to do … 11+ Maths* for step-by-step explanations and further practice.

Don't forget the website…!

Visit www.bond11plus.co.uk for lots of advice, information and suggestions on everything to do with Bond and helping children to do their best.

Key words

Some special maths words are used in this book. You will find them **in bold** each time they appear in the papers. These words are explained here.

common factors
an integer that divides exactly into two or more integers, e.g. 15 and 30 both have 3 and 5 as factors in common. Often used in simplifying fractions or equations.

coordinates
the two numbers, one horizontal, the other vertical, that plot a point on a grid, e.g. (4, 2)

cube number
a number that is multiplied by itself twice, e.g. $2^3 = 2 \times 2 \times 2$

edge
an edge is where two faces meet on a 3-D shape

face
the flat sides of a polyhedron (a solid shape with flat sides,) e.g. a cube has 6 faces

highest common factor
The highest common factor (HCF) of two numbers is found by first finding the common factors, then writing down the highest, e.g. the highest common factor of 8 and 12 is **4**

index, indices
the number of times a number is multiplied by itself, e.g. $2 \times 2 \times 2 = 2^3$ has an index of 3

integer
a positive or negative whole number, e.g. -6, 0, 3

lowest common multiple
The lowest common multiple (LCM) of two numbers is found by first finding the common multiples, then writing down the lowest, e.g. the multiples of 6 are 6, 12, 18, 24, 30, 36, 42, 48, 54, etc. The multiples of 8 are 8, 16, 24, 32, 40, 48, 56, 64, 72, etc. The common multiples of 6 and 8 are 24, 48, 72, etc. So the lowest common multiple is **24**

lowest term
the simplest you can make a fraction, e.g. $\frac{4}{10}$ reduced to the lowest term is $\frac{2}{5}$

mean
a type of average. You find the mean by adding all the scores together and dividing by the number of scores, e.g. the mean of 1, 3 and 8 is 4

median
a type of average. The middle number of a set of numbers after ordering, e.g. the median of 1, 3 and 8 is 3 e.g. the median of 7, 4, 6 and 9 is 6.5 (halfway between 6 and 7)

mixed number
a number that contains a whole number and a fraction, e.g. $5\frac{1}{2}$ is a mixed number

mode
a type of average. The most common number in a set of numbers, e.g. the mode of 2, 3, 2, 7, 2 is 2

multiple
a multiple of a number is the answer when it is multiplied by another number, e.g. 20 is a multiple of 4 and 5

parallelogram
a four-sided shape that has all its opposite sides equal and parallel

prime factor
the factors of a number that are also prime numbers, e.g. the prime factors of 12 are 2 and 3

prime number
any number that can only be divided by itself and 1, e.g. 2, 3 and 7 are prime numbers

range
the difference between the largest and smallest of a set of numbers, e.g. the range of 1, 2, 5, 3, 6, 8 is 7 (8 − 1)

scale factor
the ratio of the length of one side on one figure to the length of the corresponding side on another figure. It can relate to an enlargement or reduction in size, e.g. doubling a distance corresponds to a scale factor of 2

simultaneous equation
equations that have the same solution or solutions

square number
the square of a number is that number multiplied by itself, e.g. 3^2 is 3 'squared'; $3^2 = 3 \times 3 = 9$ therefore $3^2 = 9$

square root
any number which, when multiplied by itself, gives you the original number, e.g. 4 is the square root of 16 ($4 \times 4 = 16$; $\sqrt{16} = 4$)

vertex, vertices
the point where two or more edges or sides in a shape meet

Paper 1

Nothing after decimal needed

1–6 Round these numbers to complete the table.

	To nearest 0.1	To nearest 1	To nearest 10
109.47	109.5 ✓	109.00 ✓	110 ✗
156.85	156.9	157.00 ✓	160 ✗

B 1

4 6

7–8 Using all the digits 6 9 1 3 7 5 make: 135679   135679

the smallest possible number

the largest possible number   976531

B 1

2

9 Jack ate $\frac{1}{6}$ of a box of sweets and Jackie ate $\frac{2}{5}$ of the sweets. What fraction is left in the box?   1. Not a fraction $\frac{2.9}{6}$

B 10

1

10–15 Here is a table showing the ingredients needed to make Apple Charlotte for 4 people. Work out the ingredients needed for 10 people and complete the table.

Ingredients	For 4 people	For 10 people
Apples	450 g	1125 kg
Sugar	1 tablespoon	tablespoons
Butter	25 g	66.25 g ✓
Eggs	2	8 ✗
Bread	6 slices	15 slices ✓
Butter	80 g	160 g ✗

B25/B3

2 6

16 I think of a number, multiply it by 3, subtract 7 and then subtract the number I first thought of. The answer is 13. What was the number I first thought of? 2.855

B8/B2

B 3

17 Find the volume of a slab of marble 3 m long, 1.75 m wide and 20 cm thick. m³

B25/B22

18 If 1.5 kg of rice costs £2.40, how much will 5.5 kg cost at the same rate? £

B 3

3

19–23 Link each unit of measurement to the correct statement.

mm   capacity of a watering can
km   contents of a juice carton
gallons   thickness of a pencil lead
yards   distance from Bristol to Bath
ml   distance across a playground

B 25

5 5

A packet of fruit sweets has red, green, yellow and orange sweets in the ratio 5 : 4 : 2 : 1. Answer the following in the **lowest terms**. B13/B10 B 12

24 What fraction of the sweets are green?

25 If the packet contains 84 sweets, how many red sweets are there?

26 If half the green sweets and half the yellow sweets are eaten, what percentage of the packet remains? 3

Calculate the answers. B 11

27 $16.43 - 0.09 =$

28 $5.07 - 1.18 =$

29 $12.38 - 13.57 =$ 3

Rewrite these expressions using **common factors**. For example, $5a + 10b = 5(a + 2b)$. B8/B5

30 $4x + 16 =$

31 $6p^2 - 12p =$ 2

Simplify these expressions, using **common factors** where possible. B8/B5

32 $5a - 2b + 3a - 4b =$

33 $4x^2 - 3x + x^2 + 4x =$

34 $\frac{7x}{14} =$ 3

35–39 Complete this table of sale reductions. B11/B10

	Full price	% reduction	Sale price
Item A	£64	$12\frac{1}{2}$%	
Item B	£16.65	$33\frac{1}{3}$%	
Item C	£18.50		£14.80
Item D	£124		£93
Item E		15%	£16.15

5

Use the diagram and the information below to calculate the angles marked *a*, *b*, *c* and *d*. B18/B17

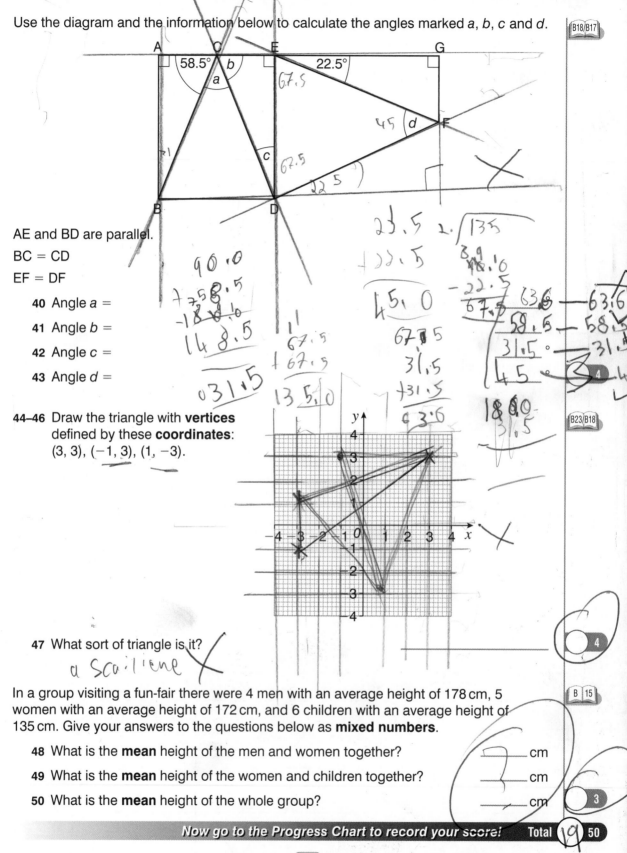

AE and BD are parallel.

BC = CD

EF = DF

40 Angle *a* =

41 Angle *b* =

42 Angle *c* =

43 Angle *d* =

44–46 Draw the triangle with **vertices** defined by these **coordinates**: (3, 3), (−1, 3), (1, −3). B23/B18

47 What sort of triangle is it?

a scailiene

In a group visiting a fun-fair there were 4 men with an average height of 178 cm, 5 women with an average height of 172 cm, and 6 children with an average height of 135 cm. Give your answers to the questions below as **mixed numbers**. B 15

48 What is the **mean** height of the men and women together? _____ cm

49 What is the **mean** height of the women and children together? _____ cm

50 What is the **mean** height of the whole group? _____ cm

Paper 2

Find the answers to these calculations.

1 $1.78 + 0.48 =$ _2.26_

2 $0.96 + 1.05 =$ _2.01_

3 $2.43 - 2.06 =$ _0.37_

4 $1.79 - 0.98 =$ _0.81_

Write in the fraction or percentage equivalents.

5 $\frac{2}{5} =$ _40_ %

6 $\frac{175}{1000} =$ _17.5_ %

7 $33\frac{1}{3}\% =$ ___

8 $5\% =$ ___

Fill in the missing numbers.

9 $1^2 + \boxed{} = 2^2$

10 $3^2 + \boxed{} = 4^2$

11 $5^2 + \boxed{} = 6^2$

12 $9^2 + \boxed{} = 10^2$

Find the given fraction of each quantity.

13 $\frac{1}{5}$ of 3 m = _60_ cm

14 $\frac{2}{3}$ of 36 kg = _24_ kg

15 $\frac{1}{6}$ of £138 = £ _23_

16 $\frac{3}{8}$ of 448 g = ___ g

17 Write $\frac{5}{8}$ as a decimal. ___

18 Write 0.32 as a fraction in its **lowest terms**. ___

19 A train travels 45 km in an hour. How many metres is that in 1 minute? ___

20 What is 13 hours 10 minutes in seconds? ___ seconds

21 In a group of 30 people, there are 18 who are 15 years of age, 9 are 16, and 3 are 17. What is the **mean** age of the group? _16_

22 What is the **mean** of this group of numbers? ___

141   193   169   155   171   155

Convert these mileages to kilometres.

23 135 miles = ___

24 38 miles = ___

25 230 miles = ___

26 12 miles = ___

Calculate the volume and surface area of each of these cuboids.

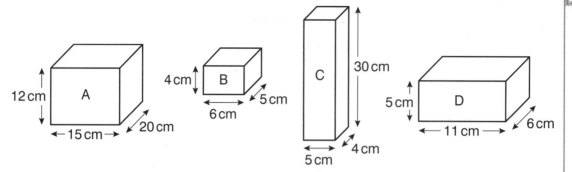

27–28 The volume of A is _____ cm³ and its surface area is _____ cm².

29–30 The volume of B is _____ cm³ and its surface area is _____ cm².

31–32 The volume of C is _____ cm³ and its surface area is _____ cm².

33–34 The volume of D is _____ cm³ and its surface area is _____ cm².

8

35–37 Use your protractor to measure these angles to the nearest degree.

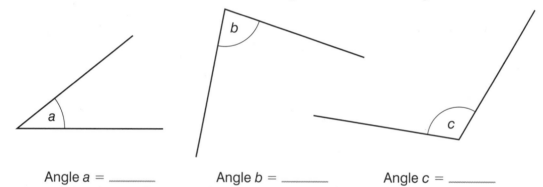

Angle a = _____   Angle b = _____   Angle c = _____

This is a temperature–time graph.

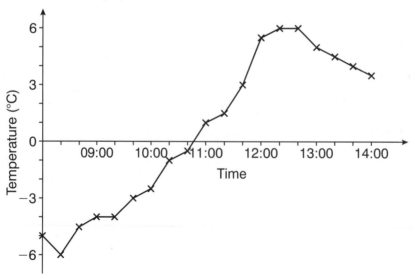

38 What was the temperature at 10:20?   ____°C

39 What was the time interval between each recording?   _____

40 How many degrees cooler was it at 08:40 than at 11:40?   ____°C

41 What is the difference between the highest and lowest temperatures?   ____°C   4

B3/B10

Use the numbers of teeth on these gear wheels to answer the questions below. Give answers as fractions in the **lowest terms**.

A   B   C

42–43 If gear A makes 5 whole turns then gear B makes ____ turns and gear C makes ____ turns.

44–45 If gear B makes 1 whole turn then gear A makes ____ turns and gear C makes ____ turn.   4

B8/B6

46–50 Complete the table of values for $y = 4 - x^2$.

x	-4	-3	-2	-1	0
y					

5

Now go to the Progress Chart to record your score!   **Total**   50

Paper 3

49   26   38   150   8   102   23   62   78   189

From this array of numbers choose those that match the terms below.

B6/B5

1 A **square number**   _____

2 A **prime number**   _____

3 A **cube number**   _____

4 A **multiple** of 9   _____

5 A **multiple** of 5   150   5

Calculate the angles marked *a*, *b* and *c*.

B17/B18

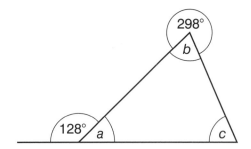

6 Angle *a* = _____

7 Angle *b* = _____

8 Angle *c* = _____

3

A bag contains 15 marbles: 7 are white, 5 are black and 3 are red. Write answers to these questions as fractions in the **lowest terms**.

B16/B10

9 What are the chances of drawing out a white marble? _____

10 What are the chances of drawing out a black marble? _____

11 What are the chances of drawing out a red marble? _____

3

Calculate the area of each of these triangles. Each small square is 2 mm × 2 mm.

B 18

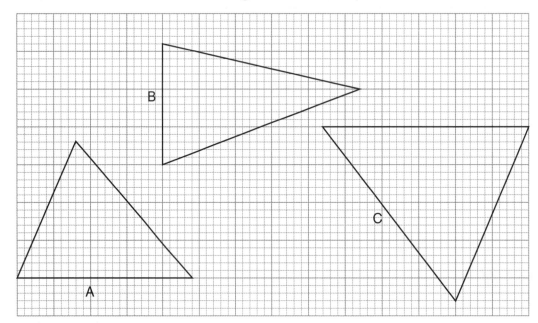

12 Area of triangle A = _____ cm²

13 Area of triangle B = _____ cm²

14 Area of triangle C = _____ cm²

3

15–19 Write these in order from smallest to largest.

0.3	$\frac{2}{7}$	25%	33%	$\frac{5}{16}$
_____	_____	_____	_____	_____

B10/B11
B 12
5

Determine the values of x, y and z.

20 $3x - 4 = 17$ $x = $ _____

21 $5y - 3 = 4y + 1$ $y = $ _____

22 $17 - 4z = 7$ $z = $ _____

B 8

Use the values you have found for x, y and z above, to calculate this expression.

23 $(2y^2 - 3x) + 2z = $ _____

4

Calculate these.

24 $2^3 \times 3^2 = $ _____   **25** $9^2 - 3^3 = $ _____

26 $4^3 - 7^2 = $ _____   **27** $3^2 + 2^4 = $ _____

B6/B3
B 2
4

Find the answers to these calculations.

28 $15.73 + 0.15 + 1.064 = $ _____

29 $107.07 + 15.47 + 2.04 = $ _____

30 $0.835 + 0.612 + 0.074 = $ _____

B 11
3

Calculate the answers to these fraction problems. Give your answers as **mixed numbers** where appropriate.

31 $\frac{1}{5} + \frac{2}{3} = $ _____   **32** $\frac{5}{8} - \frac{1}{3} = $ _____   **33** $\frac{3}{4} + \frac{4}{5} = $ _____

B 10
3

Calculate the volume of each of these cuboids.

B 22

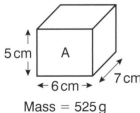

5 cm   A   7 cm   ← 6 cm →
Mass = 525 g

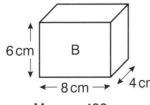

6 cm   B   4 cm   ← 8 cm →
Mass = 432 g

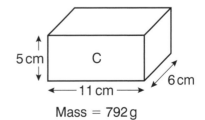

5 cm   C   6 cm   ← 11 cm →
Mass = 792 g

34 A has a volume of _____ .   **35** B has a volume of _____ .

36 C has a volume of _____ .

37–39 The density of a material is found by dividing its mass by its volume, i.e. $D = \dfrac{M}{V}$.

Put the three cuboids in order of density from least dense to most dense using A, B and C for your answers.

_____   _____   _____

Least   Most

40–43 In a survey of eye colour the following results were obtained.

Hazel	Brown	Blue	Green
25	40	30	5

Use these results, and your protractor, to complete the pie chart.

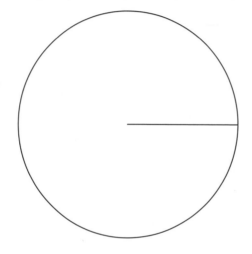

Tom chooses three numbers: −4, 2 and −5. Using these numbers find:

44 their sum.

45 their product.

$x = \frac{3}{5}$ and $y = \frac{1}{3}$. Find the value of the following, giving each answer as a fraction in **lowest terms** or a **mixed number** as appropriate.

46 $x + y =$

47 $xy =$

48 $\dfrac{x}{y} =$

Convert these areas from cm² to m².

49 33 750 cm² =

50 64 620 cm² =

6

B14/B26

4

B6/B2

B 3

2

B10/B8

3

B 25

2

Now go to the Progress Chart to record your score! Total 50

10

Paper 4

Calculate the answers to these fraction problems, giving your answers in the **lowest terms**.

1 $\frac{4}{5} + \frac{12}{30} =$

2 $\frac{7}{8} - \frac{1}{2} =$

3 $\frac{2}{3} \times \frac{1}{2} =$

4 $\frac{5}{8} \div \frac{3}{4} =$

B 10

4

5–8 Complete this table. Fractions should be in the **lowest terms**.

B10/B11

Decimal	Fraction
0.5	$\frac{1}{2}$
0.8	$\frac{1}{8}$
0.6	$\frac{1}{6}$
6.20	$\frac{4}{5}$
0.75	$\frac{3}{4}$

4

9–11 Circle the letters that have only one line of symmetry.

B 24

M B I A J N

3

12–16 Put these in order from largest to smallest.

B10/B11

0.41 $\frac{5}{12}$ $\frac{3}{8}$ 0.38 $\frac{7}{16}$

_____   _____   _____   _____   _____

5

17 Find the **HCF** of 18 and 30.

B 5

1

18   30   180   270   390   510   18   90   162   234   306   360
      60   180   300   420   540   36   108   180   252   324
      90   210   330   450   570   54   126   198   270   342
     120   240   360   480   600   72   144   216   288   360

18–20 Write 42 as a product of **prime factors**.

B5/B6

____ × ____ × ____

3

21–22 Totalling two numbers gives the answer 14. The product of the same two numbers is 48. What are the numbers?

B2/B3

6 and 8

2

Calculate the answers to these decimal problems, rounding each answer to one decimal place.

23 $13.78 + 105.83 =$ _120_ ✓

24 $26.15 \times 7 =$ _183_ ✓

25 $41.353 - 38.76 =$ _3_ ✓

26 $107.68 \div 8 =$ _13_ ✗

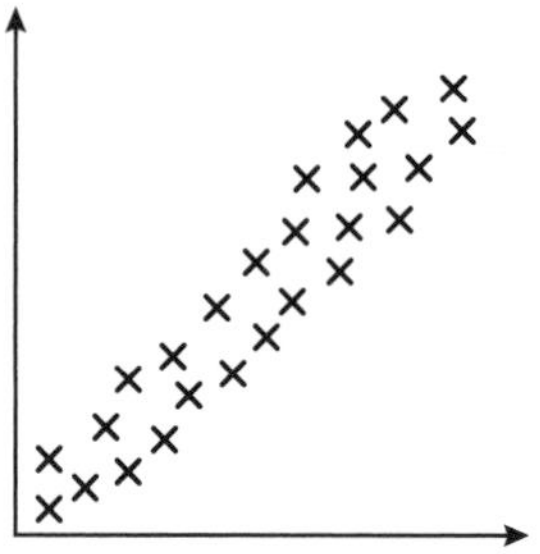

A

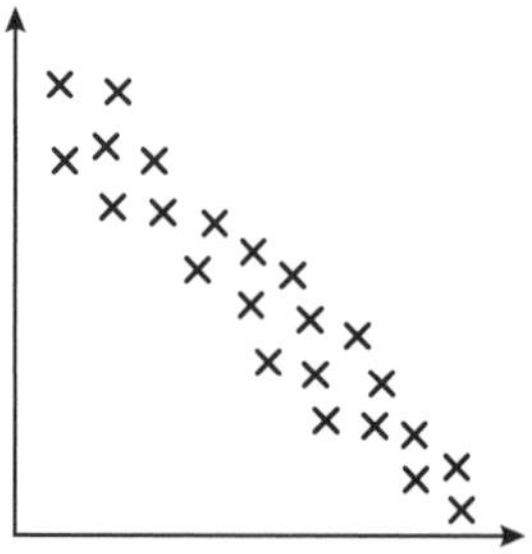

B

Handwritten working:
$$0\overset{1}{1}3.78$$
$$+ 105.83$$
$$119.6\overset{1}{1}$$

$$\overset{4}{2}6.\overset{3}{1}5 \times 7$$
$$7$$
$$183.05$$

$$3\;\overset{\cancel{1}}{\cancel{4}}.\overset{12}{8}53$$
$$-\;38.760$$
$$02.593$$

$$\overset{0\;2\;3}{8\;|\;1\,\cancel{1}\,0\cancel{7}.\cancel{3}6\cancel{8}}\quad 13.46$$

Which of these scatter graphs might show:

27 time and the value of cars? ____

28 time and the value of houses? ____

N

• Jack

Scale: 1 cm = 30 m

• Jill

◉ Oak tree

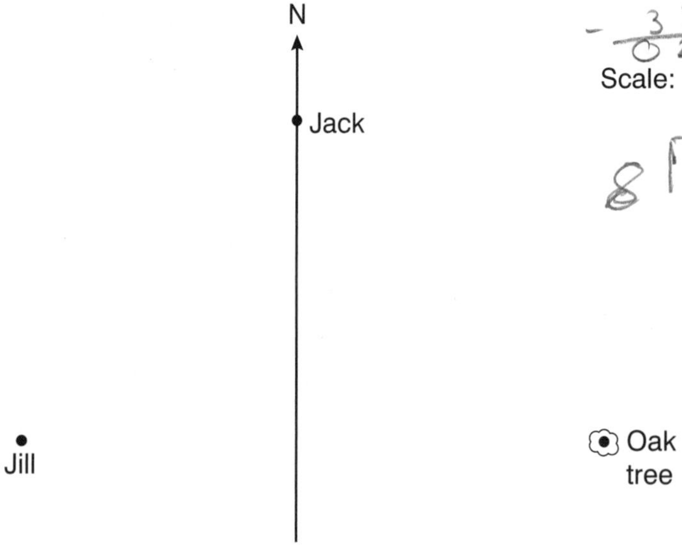

29 How far is Jack from the oak tree? _____ m

30 How far is Jill from the oak tree? _____ m

31 What bearing is the oak tree from Jill? _____ °

32 What bearing is the oak tree from Jack? _____ °

If Jack and Jill both walk towards the oak tree at 2 metres per second, how long will each take to reach the tree?

33 Jack = _____ seconds

34 Jill = _____ seconds

Name the shapes given by the following descriptions.

B 19

35 A **parallelogram** with four equal sides is a _____ .

36 A quadrilateral with one pair of parallel opposite sides is a _____ .

37 A quadrilateral with two pairs of adjacent equal sides is a _____ .

38 A rectangle with four equal sides and four equal angles is a _____ .

Complete these conversions.

B 25

39 A foot is approximately _____ mm

40 11 pounds is approximately ____ kg

41 $3\frac{1}{2}$ pints is approximately ____ litres

42 20 km is approximately _____ miles

This rectangle and triangle have the same area.

B8/B20

$(x + 2)$ cm

$(2x - 2)$ cm

3 cm

4 cm

Use the information and diagrams above to find the value of x and the area of each shape.

43 $x =$ ____

44 Area = _____

Determine the values of x.

B8/B6
B10/B11

45 $5(x - 3) = 25$ $x =$ ____

46 $4(x^2 - 8) = 32$ $x =$ ____

47 $x(3x + 3) = 6(2 + \frac{x}{2})$ $x =$ ____

48 $5(x - 1) = 2(x + 2)$ $x =$ ____

49 $\frac{1}{4}x - 0.5 = 1$ $x =$ ____

50 $\frac{2}{3}x - 5 = 3$ $x =$ ____

Now go to the Progress Chart to record your score!   Total   50

13

Paper 5

Calculate the answers to these problems.

B11/B3

1 3.74×1000 = _____   **2** 412×13 = _____

3 15×310 = _____   **4** 11×39 = _____

5 1.5×1.5 = _____   **6** 10.8×2.5 = _____

Calculate the answers to these fraction problems. Give answers in the **lowest terms**. Use **mixed numbers** where appropriate.

7 $\frac{4}{5} + \frac{4}{6} =$ _____

8 $\frac{5}{4} - \frac{2}{6} =$ _____

9 $4\frac{1}{2} + 2\frac{2}{3} =$ _____

10 $5\frac{1}{2} \times \frac{3}{4} =$ _____

11 $\frac{2}{3} \div \frac{4}{8} =$ _____

12 $5\frac{1}{2} \div 2\frac{3}{4} =$ _____

Write expressions for these.

B 8

13 The price in pence, P, of N items at 35p. $P =$ _____

14 The total cost in pence, C, of X items at £1.05 and Y items at 95p. $C =$ _____

Here are scores out of 20 for 8 students who sat a mathematics test.

B 15

13   14   10   13   16   19   13   14

15 What is the **mode**? _____

16 What is the **median**? _____

17 What is the **mean**? _____

18 What is the **range**? _____

19–22 Complete this table of dimensions of triangles.

B 18

	Height (cm)	Base (cm)	Area (cm²)
Triangle 1	8	4.5	_____
Triangle 2	7.5	6	_____
Triangle 3	4.5	_____	6.75
Triangle 4	_____	8	50

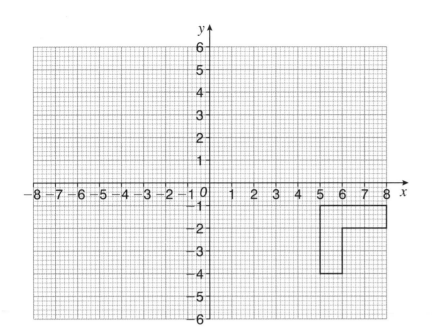

B 23

23 Translate the shape 3 units left and 5 units up.

24 Reflect the translated shape in the vertical axis.

25 Translate the last reflected shape 1 unit right and 6 units down.

26–29 Write 132 as a product of **prime factors**.

_____ × _____ × _____ × _____

B5/B6

Write the next two terms and the *n*th term for each sequence.

B7/B8

30–31   1   3   5   7   _____   _____   **32** *n*th term = _____

33–34   2   5   8   11   _____   _____   **35** *n*th term = _____

MNOP is a **parallelogram**. Calculate the angles marked *a*, *b*, *c* and *d*.

B17/B18
B 19

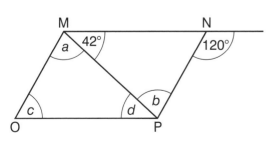

36 Angle *a* = _____°

37 Angle *b* = _____°

38 Angle *c* = _____°

39 Angle *d* = _____°

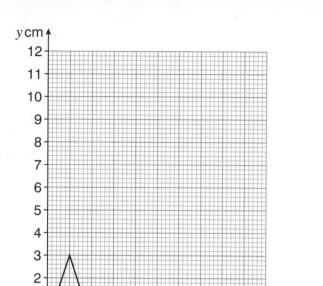

40–43 Enlarge the isosceles triangle by a **scale factor** of 3 with (0, 0) as the centre of enlargement. What are the **coordinates** of the **vertices** of the enlarged triangle?   (——— , ———) (——— , ———) and (——— , ———)

44 What is the area of the original triangle?   ——— cm²

45 What is the area of the enlarged triangle?   ——— cm²

46 How many times greater is the area of the enlarged triangle?   ———

Simplify each of these expressions.

47 $5x \times 3x - 8x^2 =$ ———————

48 $\dfrac{y}{5} + \dfrac{y}{10} =$ ———————

49 $3(s - 2t) - (2s - t) =$ ———————

50 $(4a + 2)(a - 3) =$ ———————

Now go to the Progress Chart to record your score!   Total

Paper 6

Calculate the answers to these.

1 $408 + 326 - 189 =$ _____   **2** $67 \times 38 \quad =$ _____

3 $70.2 \div 9 \qquad =$ _____   **4** $81.6 \div 12 \quad =$ _____

5 $153 \times 8 \qquad =$ _____   **6** $376 \times 204 \quad =$ _____

7 If 120 g of sweets costs 88p, how much would 270 g cost? _____ B 3

8 What is 4 weeks 2 days 11 hours in minutes? _____ minutes B27/B3

9 In a clearance sale a shirt, originally priced at £24.50, is sold for £14.70. B2/B12
What percentage discount is given? ____%

10 Calculate the **mean** for this set of numbers. B 15

$$2 \quad 12 \quad 10 \quad 7 \quad 5 \quad 9 \quad 11 \quad 8$$ _____ **4**

11–14 Circle the letters that have only one line of symmetry. B 24

K L M P T V X

4

Write each of these numbers as a product of prime factors: B5/B6

15–17 154 ____ × ____ × ____

18–20 245 ____ × ____ × ____ **6**

21–24 Complete this table by determining the values of the letters. B8/B20

B 6

	Length (cm)	Breadth (cm)	Perimeter (cm)	
Rectangle 1	$a + 4$	6	30	$a = $ ____
Rectangle 2	$2b + 3$	5	32	$b = $ ____
Rectangle 3	$c^2 - 16$	12	64	$c = $ ____
Rectangle 4	$21 - d^2$	7	38	$d = $ ____

4

25–30 Choose six of the given options to complete this decision tree. B 19

| Kite | Trapezium | Rhombus | Is it a decagon? |

SHAPES TO BE SORTED

Is it a pentagon?

Is it a quadrilateral with 4 equal sides?

25 ____

Yes / No

Does it have 1 pair of parallel sides?

26 ____   **28** ____

Yes / No   Yes / No

Does it have 4 equal angles?

Square   **27** ____   **29** ____   **30** ____

6

Use a ruler and protractor to answer the following questions.

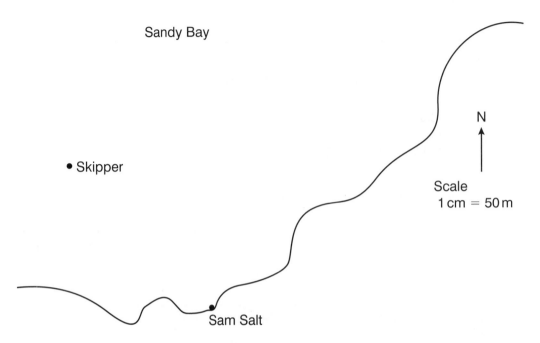

• Sally

Sandy Bay

N

• Skipper

Scale
1 cm = 50 m

Sam Salt

31 How far is Sam Salt from the boat 'Skipper'? _____ m

32 How far is Sam Salt from the boat 'Sally'? _____ m

33 How far apart are the two boats? _____ m

34 What bearing is 'Sally' from Sam? _____ °

35 What bearing is 'Skipper' from 'Sally'? _____ °

 5

From this array of numbers, choose an example that fits each description below.

> 123   63   76   17   48   27   121   58

36 A **prime number** _____

37 A **cube number** _____

38 A **square number** _____

39 A **multiple** of 7 _____

 4

Calculate the answers to these fraction problems. Give answers in the **lowest terms**. Use **mixed numbers** where appropriate.

40 $\frac{3}{4} + \frac{5}{6} + \frac{9}{12} =$ _____

41 $\frac{5}{12} - \frac{4}{15} =$ _____

42 $\frac{5}{9} \times \frac{6}{7} =$ _____

43 $\frac{4}{7} \div \frac{5}{9} =$ _____

 4

18

Here is a set of numbers:

8   36   14   9   43   22   32   40   11   25   7   35

44 What is the **mean**? ___   **45** What is the **range**? ___

46 A rectangular room contains 107.25 cubic metres of air. If the dimensions of the floor are 6.5 m and 5.5 m, what is the height of the room? ___ m

47 I think of a number, add 15, multiply by 2, then subtract the number that I first thought of. The answer is 36. What was the number I first thought of? ___

48 If 20 metres of cloth costs £64, how much will 9 metres cost? £ ___

Solve these **simultaneous equations**: $x + 5y = 13$ $3x + 7y = 23$

49 $x =$ ___   **50** $y =$ ___

Now go to the Progress Chart to record your score!   Total ◯ 50

Paper 7

Calculate the answers to these decimal problems.

1 $2.705 \times 1000 =$ ___   **2** $12.36 \div 6 =$ ___

3 $24.96 \div 3.2 =$ ___   **4** $12.4 \times 2.3 =$ ___

Using your ruler, measure the marked lengths in these triangles to the nearest mm. Then calculate the area of each triangle.

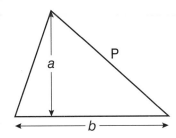
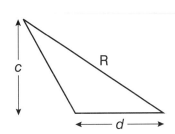

Triangle P

5 $a =$ ___ mm

6 $b =$ ___ mm

7 Area   ___ cm²

Triangle R

8 $c =$ ___ mm

9 $d =$ ___ mm

10 Area   ___ cm²

Rectangles A and B have the same area.

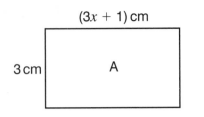

(3x + 1) cm

3 cm   A

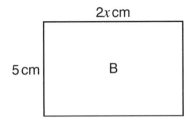

2x cm

5 cm   B

Use the information and the diagrams above to solve these problems.

11 What is the area of rectangles A and B? _____

12 What is the perimeter of rectangle A? _____

13 What is the perimeter of rectangle B? _____

14 If rectangle A was enlarged by a **scale factor** of 3, what would the enlarged area be? _____

15 If rectangle A was enlarged by a **scale factor** of 1.5, what would the enlarged area be? _____

5

B 23

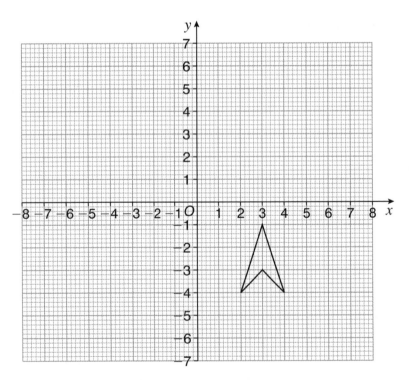

16 Reflect the shape in the horizontal axis.

17 Translate the reflected shape 6 units left and 2 units up.

18 Translate the translated shape 1 unit right and 7 units down.

3

20

Find the answers to these problems.

19 $5 - (-1.5) =$ _____

20 $17 - (-12.25) =$ _____

21 $0.5 - (-0.125) =$ _____

Calculate these fractions and percentages.

22 70% of £18 = £ _____

23 $\frac{3}{5}$ of 16 kg = _____ kg

24 85% of 48 m = _____ m

25 $\frac{1}{6}$ of £18.60 = £ _____

26 18% of $17\frac{1}{2}$ litres = _____ litres

I roll two fair, normal dice. Writing your answers as fractions in the **lowest terms**, what is the probability of getting a total of:

27 12? _____

28 7? _____

29 5? _____

30 9 or less? _____

Express the numbers below as products of **prime factors**, using **indices** where you can.

31–33 300 = ___ × ___ × ___

34–36 180 = ___ × ___ × ___

37–41 The data in this table was collected from a small group of people who were asked about the sorts of TV programmes that they preferred.

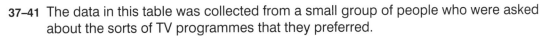

TV programme	Documentary	Comedy	News	Drama	Soaps
Number of people	18	25	7	20	2

Use the information in the table, and your protractor, to complete the pie chart.

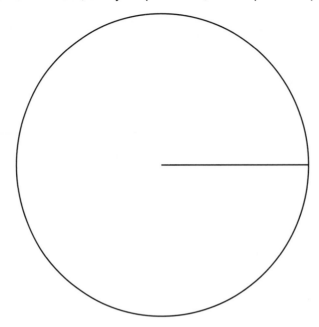

5

B8/B26

42–45 The equations for the lines on this graph are given below.

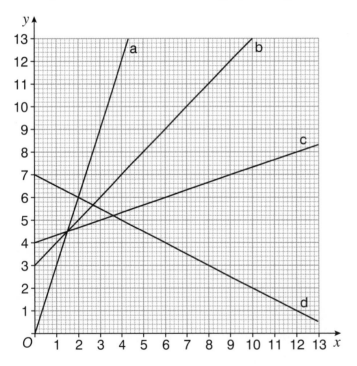

Write the letter for the appropriate line beneath each equation.

$$y = \frac{x + 12}{3} \qquad y = 3x \qquad y = x + 3 \qquad y = 7 - \tfrac{1}{2}x$$

_____   _____   _____   _____

46–48 Complete this table of values for the line with equation $x + y = 10$.

x	0	1	2	___	4
y	10	9	___	7	___

49 Draw this line on the graph above.

50 At what **coordinates** does it meet line d? (___, ___)

9

Now go to the Progress Chart to record your score!   **Total**   50

Paper 8

Calculate the answers to these problems.

1 $14.75 \times 4 =$ _____   **2** $102.02 \times 9 =$ _____   **3** $512 \times 23 =$ _____

4 $44.1 \div 7 =$ _____   **5** $122.1 \div 11 =$ _____   **6** $35.88 \div 2.3 =$ _____

6

I place 9 grey balls, 6 white balls and 5 black balls in a bag. Use this information to solve the following problems. Give fractions in the **lowest terms**.

7 What is the probability, written as a fraction, that I will draw out a black ball?   ___

8 What is the probability, written as a percentage, that I will draw out a grey ball? ___

I remove 5 balls from the bag, 2 grey, 1 white and 2 black.

9 What is the probability now, written as a fraction, that I will draw out a white ball?   ___

10 What is the probability now, written as a percentage, that I will draw out a black ball?   ___

4

Calculate the answers to these fraction problems. Give answers in the **lowest terms**. Use **mixed numbers** where appropriate.

11 $\frac{4}{7} + \frac{8}{14} =$ ___

12 $\frac{5}{8} - \frac{5}{16} =$ ___

13 $1\frac{3}{4} + 3\frac{1}{3} =$ ___

14 $\frac{3}{4} \times \frac{5}{6} \times \frac{1}{5} =$ ___

15 $6\frac{1}{2} \div 3\frac{1}{6} =$ ___

5

16–21 The table shows the numbers of birds counted on a recent field trip.

Bird	Number
Starling	30
Willow warbler	20
Blue tit	25
Martin	20
Swallow	15
Swift	10

Using the given data, and your protractor, complete the pie chart below.

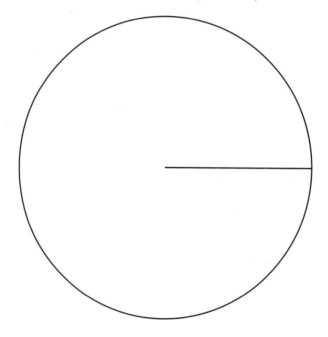

Simplify these expressions.

22 $5a + 7 - 3a + 1 =$

23 $6x + 5y - 3x + y =$

24 $4s^2 - t^2 + s^2 - 4t^2 =$

25 $3(2a - 2b) - 2(a - b) =$

26 $(3x - 1)(x + 2) =$

6

5

Calculate the surface area and volume of each of these cuboids.

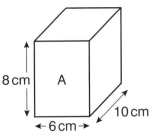

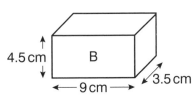

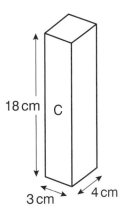

27 Cuboid A has a surface area of _____ cm².

28 Cuboid A has a volume of _____ cm³.

29 Cuboid B has a surface area of _____ cm².

30 Cuboid B has a volume of _____ cm³.

31 Cuboid C has a surface area of _____ cm².

32 Cuboid C has a volume of _____ cm³.

6

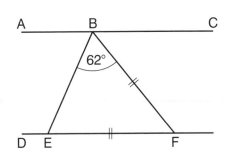

AC and DF are parallel.

BF = EF

Angle EBF = 62°

Using this information and the diagram above, calculate:

33 Angle BFE =

34 Angle BED =

35 Angle FBC =

_____ °

_____ °

_____ °

3

Rectangles A and B have the same area.

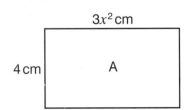

$3x^2$ cm

4 cm   A

$(x^2 + 3)$ cm

9 cm   B

Use the information given above to solve these problems.

36 What is the area of rectangles A and B?   _____

37 What is the perimeter of rectangle A?   _____

38 What is the perimeter of rectangle B?   _____   (3)

39–44 Put these in order from smallest to largest.

B10/B11

B 12

$\frac{5}{6}$ 0.89 $\frac{8}{9}$ $\frac{3}{4}$ 0.9   82%

_____   _____   _____   _____   _____   _____   (6)

Write down the next two numbers in these sequences.

B 7

45–46 17   10   3   ____   ____

47–48 $\frac{1}{16}$ $\frac{1}{4}$ 1   4   ____   ____

49–50 1   3   7   15   31   ____   ____   (6)

Now go to the Progress Chart to record your score!   Total (50)

Paper 9

Change the following decimals to fractions in the **lowest terms**.

B11/B10

1 0.625 ____   **2** 0.48 ____   **3** 0.025 ____

4 0.825 ____   **5** 0.2125 ____   (5)

Calculate these products.

B6/B3

6 $2^2 \times 3^3 =$ _____   **7** $2^3 \times 3^2 =$ _____

8 $2^2 \times 5^2 =$ _____   **9** $2^3 \times 5^2 =$ _____   (4)

26

Name these four quadrilaterals.

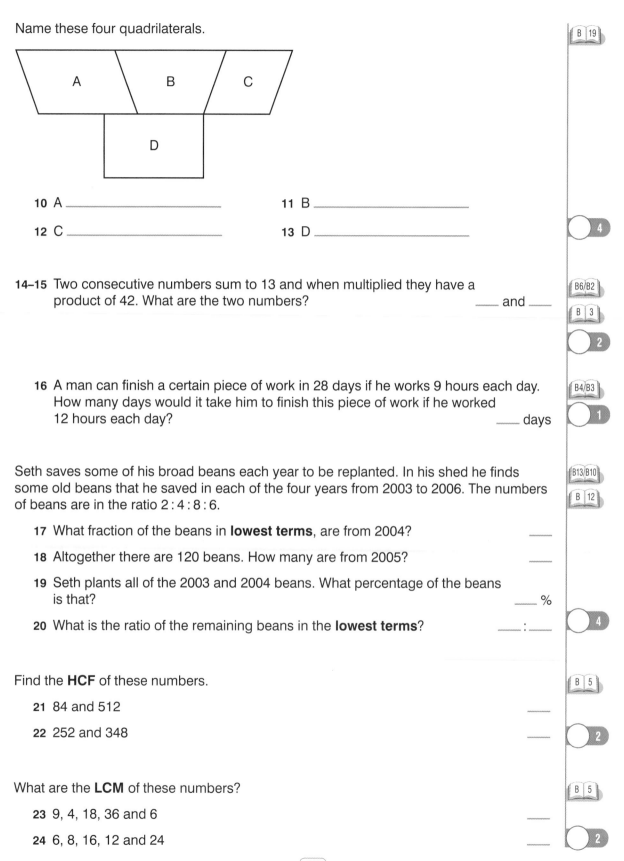

10 A _____

11 B _____

12 C _____

13 D _____

B 19

4

14–15 Two consecutive numbers sum to 13 and when multiplied they have a product of 42. What are the two numbers?   _____ and _____

B6/B2

B 3

2

16 A man can finish a certain piece of work in 28 days if he works 9 hours each day. How many days would it take him to finish this piece of work if he worked 12 hours each day?   _____ days

B4/B3

1

Seth saves some of his broad beans each year to be replanted. In his shed he finds some old beans that he saved in each of the four years from 2003 to 2006. The numbers of beans are in the ratio 2 : 4 : 8 : 6.

17 What fraction of the beans in **lowest terms**, are from 2004?   _____

18 Altogether there are 120 beans. How many are from 2005?   _____

19 Seth plants all of the 2003 and 2004 beans. What percentage of the beans is that?   _____ %

20 What is the ratio of the remaining beans in the **lowest terms**?   _____ : _____

B13/B10

B 12

4

Find the **HCF** of these numbers.

21 84 and 512   _____

22 252 and 348   _____

B 5

2

What are the **LCM** of these numbers?

23 9, 4, 18, 36 and 6   _____

24 6, 8, 16, 12 and 24   _____

B 5

2

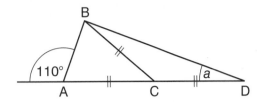

AC = BC = CD

25 Using the information in the diagram above, calculate angle *a*. _____

26 Mark in an arrow for north, which points in the direction of the negative *x*-axis. Plot the point, A, with **coordinates** (2, 2).

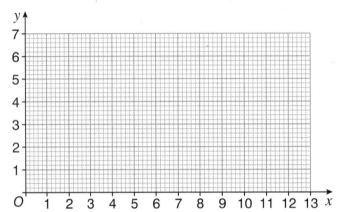

27 From A, on a bearing of 135°, draw a line that ends when *x* = 5.
What are the **coordinates** of this end-point, B? (___, ___)

28 From B, draw a line that goes 4 units south.
What are the **coordinates** of the end-point, C, of this line? (___, ___)

29 From C, on a bearing of 225°, draw a line that ends at *y* = 2.
What are the **coordinates** of this end-point, D? (___, ___)

30 Draw a line back to your starting point. What shape have you made?
_____

The contents of this can of cooking sauce are put into the rectangular-based oven dish.

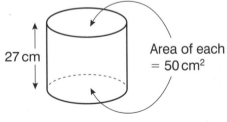

Area of each = 50 cm²

Circumference = 25 cm

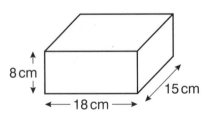

31 What is the volume of the can? _____

32 What is the capacity of the dish? _____

33 What fraction of the dish, expressed in **lowest terms**, does the contents of the can fill? _____

34 What is the surface area of the dish (it has no lid)? _____

35 What was the surface area of the can before it was opened? _____

Solve these **simultaneous equations**.

36–37 $2x + 4y = 14$ and $4x - 2y = 8$ $\qquad x =$ _____ $y =$ _____

38–39 $4x + y = 13$ and $6x - 5y = 13$ $\qquad x =$ _____ $y =$ _____

40–41 $x + y = 17$ and $x - y = 3$ $\qquad x =$ _____ $y =$ _____

Calculate the answers to these problems, giving your answers as fractions in the **lowest terms**.

42 Multiply $2\frac{5}{6}$ by 3. _____

43 Multiply $1\frac{13}{14}$ by 7. _____

44 Divide $17\frac{7}{9}$ by 8. _____

45 Divide $15\frac{5}{9}$ by 8. _____

Simplify these expressions.

46 $x^3 \div x =$ _____

47 $2a^2 \div a^2 =$ _____

Simplify these expressions.

48 $\dfrac{3ab}{a} =$ _____

49 $\dfrac{5a^2}{15ab^2} =$ _____

50 $(2a + 5b) - (a - 2b) =$ _____

Now go to the Progress Chart to record your score! **Total** 50

Paper 10

Calculate the answers to these fraction problems. Give answers in the **lowest terms**. Use **mixed numbers** where appropriate.

1 $\frac{5}{9} \times \frac{6}{7} =$ _____

2 $\frac{5}{12} \times 4 =$ _____

3 $\frac{5}{8} \times \frac{2}{5} \times \frac{4}{7} =$ _____

4 $\frac{1}{3} \div \frac{2}{3} =$ _____

5 $1\frac{1}{8} \div 1\frac{1}{2} =$ _____

6 $\frac{3}{14} \div \frac{2}{7} =$ _____

29

Use the rules for brackets to calculate or simplify these.

7 $18 \div (9 - (6 - 3)) + 5 =$ _____

8 $(x + 3)(x + 4) =$ _____

9 $(a + 2b)(a - 2b) =$ _____

10 $(a + b + c) - (a - b + c) =$ _____

11 $3(x^2 - 5x) - 2(x^2 - 5x) =$ _____

12 $x(x - y) + y(x + y) =$ _____

B8/B6

○ 6

Calculate the answers to these.

13 $(-2) + (-9) =$ _____

14 $8 - (-1) =$ _____

15 $(-15) + (-11) =$ _____

B6/B2

○ 3

Express each of these ratios in its simplest form.

16 16 to 8 _____

17 $7\frac{3}{4}$ to $15\frac{1}{2}$ _____

18 $4\frac{1}{2}$ to 18 _____

B13/B10

○ 3

19 The ratio $x : 68$ is equivalent to the ratio $3 : 4$. What is x? _____

B 13

20 What must the first term of a sequence be, if the next four terms are
$\frac{1}{18}, \frac{1}{12}, \frac{1}{9}, \frac{5}{36}$? _____

B7/B10

○ 2

Continue each of these sequences.

21–22 1   4   9   16   ____   ____

23–24 −1   2   7   14   ____   ____

B 7

○ 4

25–27 The first of three numbers is double the second, the second is double the third, and the **mean** of the three numbers is 77. What are the numbers?

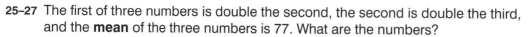

____ , ____ and ____

B13/B15

○ 3

28 If 14 m of cloth costs £24, how much does 70 m of the same cloth cost?   £ _____

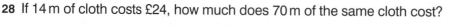

B 3

○ 1

The **mean** of five numbers is 68. Four of the numbers are 42, 39, 84 and 76.

29 What is the **mean** of the three largest numbers? _____

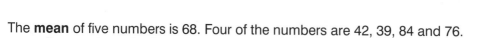

30 What is the **mean** of the three smallest numbers? _____

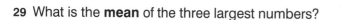

B 15

○ 2

31–34 Use this graph to draw lines that relate to the equations below. Label the lines A, B, C and D.

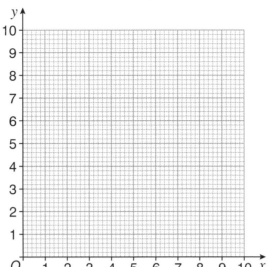

The equation for A is $y = 3x$

The equation for B is $y = x + 1$

The equation for C is $y = 4 - \frac{1}{2}x$

The equation for D is $y = \dfrac{x + 8}{2}$

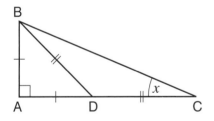

AB = AD

BD = CD

35 Using the information in the diagram above, calculate the angle x. _____

How many minutes are in

36 0.6 of an hour? _____ minutes

37 a fortnight? _____ minutes

38 three weeks, five days, four hours? _____ minutes

Calculate the answers to these.

39 $3.61 \times 2.5 =$ _____

40 $0.23 \times 0.21 =$ _____

41 $3.28 \times 9.1 =$ _____

42 $16.79 \div 7.3 =$ _____

43 $7.02 \div 1.95 =$ _____

44 $106.2 \div 4.5 =$ _____

B8/B10

B 26

4

B17/B18

1

B 27

3

B 11

6

For any size of circle: $\dfrac{\text{circumference}}{\text{diameter}} = \pi$.

Take π to be 3.14.

A wheel has a diameter of 90 cm.

B17/B25
B 3

45 If I roll it for one complete turn, how far has the wheel travelled? _____ cm

46 If the wheel moves 4.239 m, how many turns has it made? ____

2

47–50 Complete this table, which is about rectangular shapes.

B 20

Length (cm)	Breadth (cm)	Area (cm²)	Perimeter (cm)
15	____	97.5	43
____	7.5	63.75	32
20	9.25	____	58.5
12	5.5	66	____

4

Now go to the Progress Chart to record your score!   **Total**   **50**

Paper 11

Calculate the answers to these.

B6/B2
B 3

1 $0 - (-2) = $ ____

2 $(-3) - (-2) = $ ____

3 $2 - (-10) = $ ____

4 $3 \times (-10) = $ ____

5 $(-1)(-3) = $ ____

6 $(-1)^2 = $ ____

6

Calculate these fractions and percentages.

B10/B12

7 $6\frac{1}{2}\%$ of £300 = £ _____

8 A boy spends 30% of his pocket money and has £3.50 left.
How much did he have to start with? £ _____

9 Find $\frac{7}{11}$ of £6.05. £ _____

10 What is $2\frac{8}{9}$ of £2.70? £ _____

4

Use the diagram of the clock face to help you work out the angle between the two minute hands for each pair of times.

B17/B27

11 11:15 a.m. and 2:45 p.m.

12 9:20 p.m. and 1:35 a.m.

13 12:30 p.m. and 12:35 p.m.

_____ °

_____ °

_____ °

3

Calculate the answers to these.

14 $(7 + (9 - (8 - 3))) =$ _____

15 $(9 - (7 - (6 - 5))) =$ _____

16 $(5 - 3)(7 - 4) =$ _____

17 $(7 \times 6) - (4 \times 2) + (16 \div 2) =$ _____

Simplify these expressions.

18 $7(3a - 2b + 3c) - 4(a - 3b + 5c) =$ _____

19 $4(5x - 3y) - 3(2x + 3y) =$ _____

20 $2a(a - b) + 2ab =$ _____

Use the information given in the diagrams to answer the questions that follow. The shapes in each pair have the same area.

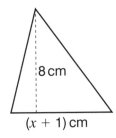

3 cm

$(2x - 2)$ cm

21 What is the area of each shape? _____

22 What is the perimeter of the rectangle? _____

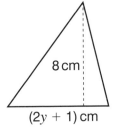

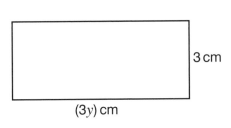

3 cm

$(3y)$ cm

23 What is the area of each shape? _____

24 What is the perimeter of the rectangle? _____

Express the numbers below as products of **prime factors**, using **indices** where you can.

25–27 $5445 =$ ___ × ___ × ___

28–30 $1683 =$ ___ × ___ × ___

33

A woman has a yearly net income of £24 000. She saves $\frac{1}{6}$ of it. Of the remainder, she pays 25% in rent, 20% on other bills and spends the rest.

31 How much does she save?　　　　　　　　　　　　　£ _____

32 How much is the annual rent?　　　　　　　　　　　£ _____

33 What does she spend?　　　　　　　　　　　　　　£ _____

Calculate the answers to these fraction problems. Give answers in the **lowest terms**. Use **mixed numbers** where appropriate.

34 $7\frac{13}{28} + 6\frac{29}{42} =$　　　　　　　　　　　_____

35 $3\frac{7}{9} - 2\frac{13}{18} =$　　　　　　　　　　　_____

36 $3\frac{4}{7} + 6\frac{5}{6} - \frac{2}{3} =$　　　　　　　_____

37 $1\frac{5}{6} \times \frac{2}{3} =$　　　　　　　　　　　_____

38 $1\frac{7}{9} \div \frac{1}{3} =$　　　　　　　　　　　_____

Solve these **simultaneous equations**.

39–40 $x - 3y = -1$ and $2x - 4y = 2$　　　　　$x =$ ___ 　$y =$ ___

41–42 $x - 2y = 0$ and $4x + 3y = 11$　　　　　$x =$ ___ 　$y =$ ___

A group of students were asked to think of a number between 0 and 80. This table shows the numbers that they thought of.

17	60	23	12	5	37
33	28	42	73	67	3
46	77	19	57	48	38
29	30	38	57	67	36
70	31	45	11	22	40
53	37	67	13	44	73

43–46 Complete this frequency table.

Numbers	0–19	20–39	40–59	60–79
Frequency	_____	_____	_____	_____

47–50 Draw a bar chart to show the grouped data in the frequency table.

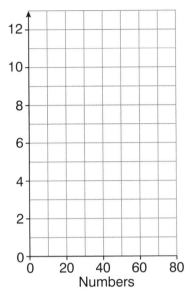

Numbers

○ 8

Now go to the Progress Chart to record your score!   Total ○ 50

Paper 12

1–6 Complete this table.

	×0.1	×10	×100
0.0638			
0.001 04			

B 1

○ 6

Calculate these percentages.

B 12

7 $2\frac{1}{4}$% of £200 =   £ _____

8 15% of £96 =   £ 6.40p ✓

9 $\frac{3}{4}$% of £8 =   200p p

10 $7\frac{1}{2}$% of £16 =   £ _____

○ 4

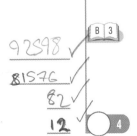

Calculate the answers to these.

B 3

11 671 × 138 =   92598 ✓

12 618 × 132 =   81576 ✓

13 9594 ÷ 117 =   82 ✓

14 8100 ÷ 675 =   12

○ 4

35

Solve these equations.

15 $80 - 32t = -80$ $t = $ _____

16 $n - (2n - 1) = 5 - 2(n - 1)$ $n = $ _____

17 $x - \dfrac{30x}{100} = 35$ $x = $ _____

18 $\dfrac{5}{y} + \dfrac{3}{7} = \dfrac{41}{14}$ $y = $ _____   4

In my village the ratio of children to adults is $3 : 4$. There are 678 children and the ratio of girls to boys is $2 : 1$.

B 13

19 How many adults are there?   _____

20 How many girls are there?   _____   2

B 23

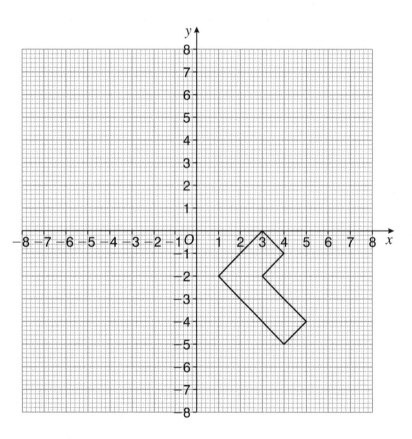

21 Reflect this shape in the horizontal axis.

22 Translate the reflected shape 6 units left and 1 unit up.

23 Reflect the translated shape in the horizontal axis.   3

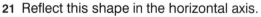

The diagram shows part of an ornamental garden. All of the paths are 2 m wide and the flower beds are the same shape and size.

B20/B3

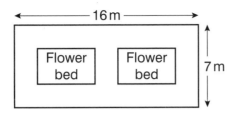

24 What is the total area of the flower beds? _____ m²

25 What is the total area of the path? _____ m²

26 Square paving stones with sides 50 cm long are laid on the paths.
How many paving stones are needed to completely pave the paths? _____

3

27–32 This chart shows distances between places in miles. Convert it to a chart showing distances in kilometres. Round your answers to the nearest kilometre.

B 25

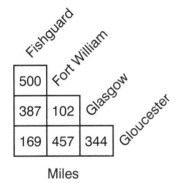

Miles

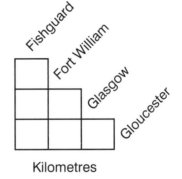

Kilometres

6

This is a regular decagon (ten sides). Calculate the marked angles.

B17/B18
B 19

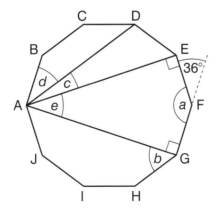

33 a = _____   34 b = _____

35 c = _____   36 d = _____

37 e = _____

5

37

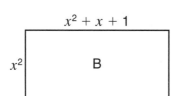

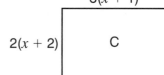

$x^2 - 1$

$2x - 1$ | **A**

$x^2 + x + 1$

x^2 | **B**

$3(x + 1)$

$2(x + 2)$ | **C**

A has a perimeter of 26 cm.

B has a perimeter of 44 cm.

C has a perimeter of 44 cm.

Using the diagrams and the information given above, calculate the area of each rectangle.

38 Area of rectangle A = _____

39 Area of rectangle B = _____

40 Area of rectangle C = _____

You are going to draw graphs of $y = 4 - x$ and $y = 2x + 1$ on the grid below. When plotting your axes, make sure they extend to include negative numbers to at least $x = -4$.

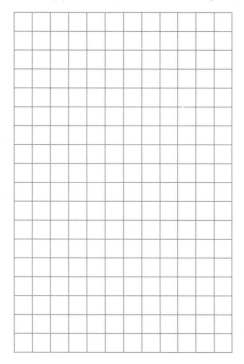

41–42 Draw and label appropriate axes on the grid.

43 Plot the graph of $y = 4 - x$.

44 Now plot the graph of $y = 2x + 1$.

45 Write the **coordinates** of the point where the two lines intersect. (___, ___)

Simplify these expressions.

46 $\dfrac{x}{y} \div \dfrac{x}{z} =$ _____

47 $\dfrac{a}{b} \times \dfrac{c}{a} =$ _____

48 $(x^2 - 2x) \div x =$ _____

Solve these **simultaneous equations**.

$$5(x - 1) + 2(y + 1) = 42 \qquad x = 2y - 3$$

49 $x =$ _____

50 $y =$ _____

Now go to the Progress Chart to record your score!　Total　50

Paper 13

Calculate these **square numbers**.

1 $11^2 =$ _____　　**2** $13^2 =$ _____　　**3** $16^2 =$ _____　　**4** $21^2 =$ _____

Calculate these **square roots**.

5 $\sqrt{81}$ = _____

6 $\sqrt{196}$ = _____

7 $\sqrt{324}$ = _____

8 $\sqrt{900}$ = _____

Express the numbers below as products of **prime factors**, using **indices** where you can.

9–10 $40 =$ _____ × _____

11–13 $252 =$ _____ × _____ × _____

Calculate the answers to these.

14 $(-13) - 13 =$ _____

15 $(-11) - (-11) =$ _____

16 $-18 - (-10) =$ _____

Calculate these percentages.

17 63% of £156 = £ _____

18 48% of £250 = £ _____

19 27% of £320 = £ _____

20 13% of £375 = £ _____

Reduce these fractions to their **lowest terms**, using **mixed numbers** where appropriate.

B 10

21 $\frac{94}{235}$ = _____   **22** $\frac{162}{243}$ = _____

4

23 $\frac{27}{18}$ = _____   **24** $\frac{132}{48}$ = _____

Fill in the gaps in these.

B 8

25 $a - 2b - 2c = a - 2(\underline{\hspace{2cm}})$

26 $p - q + r = p - (\underline{\hspace{2cm}})$

27 $x^2 - xy = x(\underline{\hspace{2cm}})$

4

28 $l + m - n = m - (\underline{\hspace{2cm}})$

29–33 Put these in order from smallest to largest.

B10/B11
B 12
5

$\frac{5}{12}$ 0.45   40% $\frac{4}{9}$ 0.39

_____   _____   _____   _____   _____

B23/B21
B18/B3

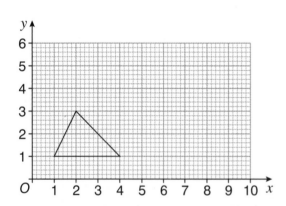

34–36 Enlarge the triangle by a **scale factor** of 2 with (0, 0) as the centre of enlargement. What are the **coordinates** of the **vertices** of the enlarged triangle?

(___ , ___) (___ , ___) (___ , ___)

Given that each small square represents $2\,mm^2$, what is the area, in centimetres of:

37 the original triangle?   ___

38 the enlarged triangle?   ___

39 How many times greater is the enlarged area?   ___

6

Calculate the answers to these decimal problems, rounding answers to two decimal places.

B11/B1

40 7.132×4 = _____   **41** 1.342×9 = _____

42 $9.51 \div 6$ = _____   **43** $3.234 \div 3$ = _____

44 6.47×1.5 = _____   **45** 3.72×3.3 = _____

6

46–48 Complete this table of values for $y = 3 - \dfrac{x}{2}$.

x	0	1	2	3	4	5	6	7	8	9
y	3	___	2	$1\frac{1}{2}$	1	$\frac{1}{2}$	___	$-\frac{1}{2}$	-1	___

B8/B10

◯ 3

49–50 Using the values in the table above, mark appropriate scales and draw the line $y = 3 - \dfrac{x}{2}$ on this graph paper.

B26B14

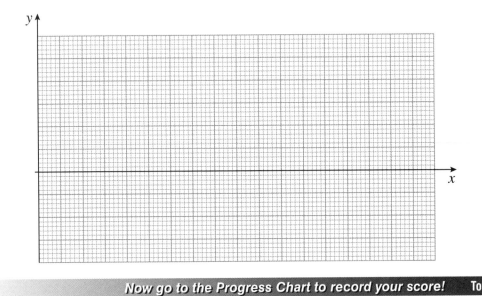

◯ 2

Now go to the Progress Chart to record your score!   **Total** ◯ 50

Paper 14

In this collection of numbers identify:

B6/B5

1 a **prime number** _____

2 a **cube number** _____

3 a **square number** _____

4 a **multiple** of 9 _____

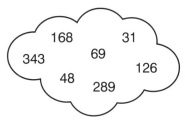

168   31
343   69
48   126
289

◯ 4

Fill in the missing number in each of these.

B6/B2

B 3

5        $-1 \times$ ____ $+ 6 = 10$

6        $3 \times$ ____ $- 20 = -2$

7        $-7 \times$ ____ $- 30 = 5$

◯ 3

41

Every card in a deck of 52 playing cards has an equal chance of being selected. Giving answers as fractions in the **lowest terms**, find the probability of selecting:

8 a red card   ____

9 a picture card   ____

10 the Jack of Spades   ____

11 an Ace   ____

B16/B10

4

Calculate the answers to these fraction problems. Give answers in the **lowest terms**. Use **mixed numbers** where appropriate.

B 10

12 $\frac{1}{4} + \frac{3}{8} + \frac{23}{24} =$ _____

13 $12\frac{1}{2} - 9\frac{3}{4} =$ _____

14 $\frac{4}{7} \times \frac{7}{9} =$ _____

15 $3\frac{3}{4} \times 3\frac{2}{5} =$ _____

16 $\frac{4}{7} \div \frac{8}{9} =$ _____

17 $\frac{8}{9} \div \frac{2}{3} =$ _____

6

Calculate the angles marked a, b, c and d.

B17/B18

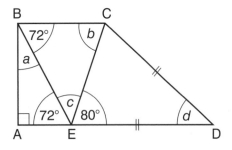

$CD = ED$

18 Angle $a =$ ____ °

19 Angle $b =$ ____ °

20 Angle $c =$ ____ °

21 Angle $d =$ ____ °

4

Calculate the answers to these problems.

B 11

22 $12.6 \times 13.2 =$ ____

23 $60.2 \times 32.5 =$ ____

24 $98.4 \div 0.8 =$ ____

25 $238.5 \div 0.9 =$ ____

26 $150.2 \times 2.5 =$ ____

4

27–31 What is the order of rotational symmetry of these shapes?

B 24

____   ____   ____   ____   ____

6

What is the **LCM** of:

B 5

32 6, 8, 16, 12 and 24? ____

33 9, 4, 18, 36 and 6? ____

What is the **HCF** of:

B 5

34 72 and 120? ____

35 105, 135 and 180? ____

4

Calculate the volume and surface area of each of these cuboids.

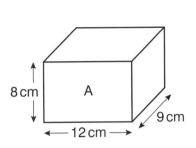

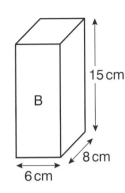

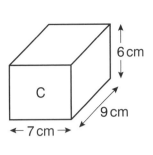

36–37 A has a volume of _____ and a surface area of _____ .

38–39 B has a volume of _____ and a surface area of _____ .

40–41 C has a volume of _____ and a surface area of _____ .

6

Solve these equations.

B 8

42 $3r + 2 = 5r - 1$ $r =$ ___

43 $p = 2(p - 3)$ $p =$ ___

44 $10(x + 4) - 7(x - 3) = 100$ $x =$ ___

3

Solve these **simultaneous equations**.

B 8

$$3x - 2y = 6 \qquad x + 3y = 13$$

45 $x =$ ___   **46** $y =$ ___

2

47–50 We collected the following data after conducting a recent survey of the trees in our village. Use these results, and your protractor, to complete the pie chart.

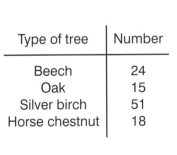

Type of tree	Number
Beech	24
Oak	15
Silver birch	51
Horse chestnut	18

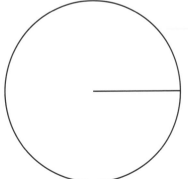

4

Now go to the Progress Chart to record your score!   **Total**   50

Paper 15

1–4 Round these numbers to complete the table.

	Rounded to nearest 0.1	Rounded to nearest 10
9.65	_____	_____
105.77	_____	_____

4

Complete these sequences.

B7/B10

5–6 $\frac{7}{8}$ $\frac{14}{16}$ _____ $\frac{56}{64}$ _____

7–8 1   _____   27   64   _____

4

Calculate the answers to these.

B2/B3

B 8

9 $(5 \times 7) + (3 \times 4) - 4 =$ _____   **10** $5 \times (7 + 3) \times (4 - 4) =$ _____

2

Solve these equations.

B 8

11 $5x + 11 = 2x + 23$ $x =$ _____   **12** $\frac{x}{3} - 2 = \frac{3x}{4} - \frac{x}{2}$ $x =$ _____

13 $6(2x - 7) = 5(5x - 11)$ $x =$ _____   **14** $\frac{1}{3}(x + 1) - \frac{1}{5}(x - 5) = 0$ $x =$ _____

4

Put one of these signs $<$, $>$ or $=$ in each of these statements to make them correct.

15 $5^3 \div 5$ _____ $4^2 + 2^3$

B 6

16 $150 \div 4$ _____ 18.75×2

B 11

17 $11.5 - 20.5$ _____ $^-3 \times {}^-3$

B11/B6

18 $(226 + 15) - (7 \times 6)$ _____ $(99 + 1) + (49 \times 2)$

B2/B3

19 $9^2 - 3.5$ _____ 10.5×7

B6/B11

20 $3^3 \times 2$ _____ 9×6

B3/B6

6

Use a protractor to measure these angles to the nearest degree, and then write in whether the angle is acute, obtuse or reflex.

B26/B17

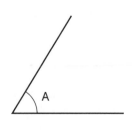

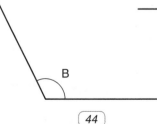

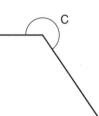

21–22 Angle A is _____° and is an _____ angle.

23–24 Angle B is _____° and is an _____ angle.

25–26 Angle C is _____° and is a _____ angle.

27–30 Calculate, to two decimal places, the **mean** number of runs per wicket for these local bowlers.

Bowler	Runs	Wickets	Average
Porter	2466	147	_____
Mann	1153	75	_____
Halton	1878	128	_____
Kent	1095	62	_____

Name the shapes.

 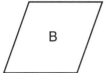 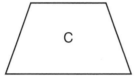  

31 A _____

32 B _____

33 C _____

34 D _____

35 E _____

36–40 Put these in order from largest to smallest.

76% $\frac{25}{32}$ 0.74 0.751 $\frac{3}{4}$

_____ _____ _____ _____ _____

41–44 Complete this table of values for $y = \frac{x}{2} + \frac{3}{2}$.

x	0	1	2	3	4
y	$\frac{3}{2}$	____	____	____	____

45 Plot the graph of $y = \dfrac{x}{2} + \dfrac{3}{2}$ using the values from the table.

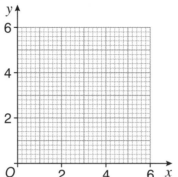

B14/B26

○ 5

For any size of circle: $\dfrac{\text{circumference}}{\text{diameter}} = \pi$

B 17

Take π to be 3.14.

Calculate the radius for each of these.

46 A circle has a circumference of 31.4 cm. What is its radius? _____

47 A circle has a circumference of 75.36 m. What is its radius? _____

48 A circle has a circumference of 94.2 mm. What is its radius? _____

49 A circle has an area of 113.04 cm². What is its radius? _____

50 A circle has an area of 530.66 km². What is its radius? _____

○ 5

Now go to the Progress Chart to record your score!   **Total** ○ 50

Paper 16

Look at this part of a number pattern.

B7/B6

$3^2 + 7 = 16 = 4^2$

$4^2 + 9 = 25 = 5^2$

$5^2 + 11 = 36 = 6^2$

Use this to complete the next two lines:

1–3 $6^2 +$ ___ $=$ ___ $=$ ___   **4–6** $7^2 +$ ___ $=$ ___ $=$ ___

○ 6

Calculate the answers to these.

B6/B2

7 $18 - (-11) =$ _____   **8** $(-2) - 20 =$ _____

9 $40 - (-20) =$ _____   **10** $-12 - (-7) =$ _____

○ 4

Reduce these fractions to their **lowest terms** using **mixed numbers** as appropriate.

B 10

11 $\dfrac{60}{96} =$ _____   **12** $\dfrac{132}{48} =$ _____

13 $\dfrac{120}{45} =$ _____   **14** $\dfrac{105}{1155} =$ _____

○ 4

Work out the approximate equivalents for these distances.

B 25

15 64 km = _____ miles

16 115 miles = _____ km

2

Express the numbers below as products of **prime factors**, using **indices** where you can.

B5/B6

17–18 52 = ____ × ____

19–20 54 = ____ × ____

21–23 126 = ____ × ____ × ____

7

Rectangles A, B and C have the same area.

B8/B20

$(x + 1)$ | A | x^4

x^2 | B | $3x^2$

$3x$ | C | $4x$

Use the diagrams and information given above to solve the following problems.

24 $x =$ ____

25 The perimeter of A is ____ cm.

26 The perimeter of B is ____ cm.

27 The perimeter of C is ____ cm.

4

Use your protractor and ruler to answer these.

B26/B17

Give the bearings of each of the boats from the buoy to the nearest degree.

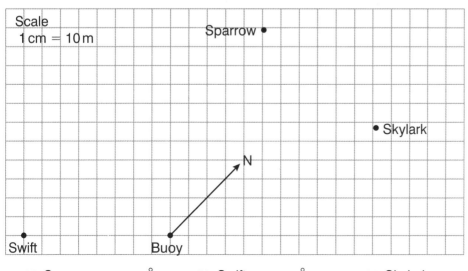

Scale
1 cm = 10 m

Sparrow

Skylark

N

Swift   Buoy

28 Sparrow _____ °   **29** Swift _____ °   **30** Skylark _____ °

Give the distances between the pairs of boats to the nearest metre.

31 Swift and Sparrow   _____

32 Sparrow and Skylark   _____

33 Swift and Skylark   _____

34 What is the bearing of Sparrow from Skylark?   _____ °

Simplify these expressions.

35 $4y - (x - 3y) =$ _____   **36** $p - 3(r - p) =$ _____

37 $yz - z(y - z) =$ _____   **38** $(4a^2 - 6ab) \div 2a =$ _____

39 How many metres are there in 12.25 km?   _____ m

I rolled a fair dice twenty times and got these scores:

1	3	2	5	1	3	3	4	5	2
2	4	5	4	3	5	1	6	6	5

40–45 Complete this frequency table.

Score	Frequency
1	
2	
3	
4	
5	
6	

46 What is the **mean** score?   _____

47–50 This table shows the heating sources for a sample of homes.

Fuel	Percentage of homes
Wood	18%
Gas	16%
Oil	39%
Electricity	27%

Complete this pie chart, using the given data. Round the angles to the nearest degree.

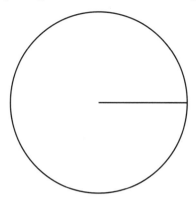

Now go to the Progress Chart to record your score!   Total 50

4

Paper 17

Multiply each of these by one thousand.

B 1

1 2.74 _____   2 1.08   _____

3 0.953 _____   4 0.075 18 _____

4

Calculate the answers to these.

B2/B3

5 Add together 534, 4397 and 61.   _____

6 Add together 184, 392 and 571.   _____

7 Take 1896 from 3203.   _____

8 Take 2193 from 7061.   _____

9 Multiply 536 by $5\frac{1}{2}$.   _____

10 Divide 7956 by 6.   _____ 6

Calculate these fractions and percentages.

B12/B10

11 30% of £15 =   £ _____   12 $\frac{4}{9}$ of £63.09 =   £ _____

13 65% of £32.60 = £ _____   14 $\frac{3}{11}$ of £143.11 = £ _____ 4

If $x = 6$, what are the values of these? Give fractions in the **lowest terms**.

B10/B8

B 6

15 $\dfrac{2x}{15}$ = ___   16 $\frac{1}{2}x^2$ = ___   17 $x^2 - 5x$ = ___

3

49

If $a = 3$ and $b = 5$, what are the values of these?

18 $2a - b =$ _____   **19** $ba^2 =$ _____   **20** $\dfrac{2a}{b} =$ _____

Calculate the areas of these **parallelograms** and triangles. Each small square represents 2 mm by 2 mm.

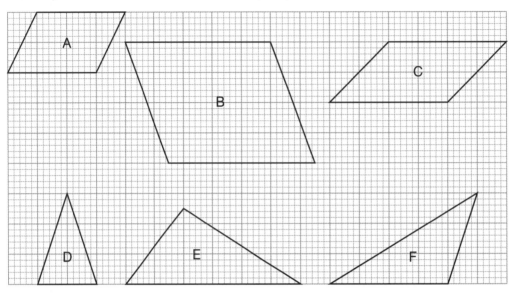

21 A = _____ cm²   **22** B = _____ cm²

23 C = _____ cm²   **24** D = _____ cm²

25 E = _____ cm²   **26** F = _____ cm²

One number is chosen at random from 1, 2, 3, 4, 5, 6, 7 and 8. Writing your answers as fractions in the **lowest terms**, work out the probability of the number being:

27 even   _____

28 a **prime number**   _____

29 divisible by 3   _____

30–33 In a local shop there is a sale. Different items have different reductions. Complete this table to show reductions and sale prices.

Percentage off	Full price	Reduction	Sale price
$12\frac{1}{2}\%$	£130	£ _____	£ _____
$7\frac{1}{2}\%$	£92	£ _____	£ _____

Express the numbers below as products of **prime factors**, using **indices** where you can.

B5/B6

34–35 245 = _____ × _____

36–37 363 = _____ × _____

38–40 294 = _____ × _____ × _____

  41 256 = _____

8

Look at this sequence: 1   3   5   7

B 7

  42 What is the 15th term in this sequence? _____

  43 What is the 100th term in this sequence? _____

2

44–45 Complete this table of values for $y = x^2 + 2x$.

B8/B14

B26/B23

x	0	1	2	3	4	5	6
y	0	3	8	15	_____	_____	48

  46 Plot the graph of $y = x^2 + 2x$ using the values in the table.

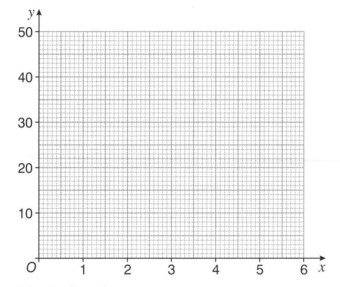

47–48 Complete this table of values for $y = 37 - 5x$.

x	0	1	2	3	4	5	6
y	37	32	27	_____	_____	12	7

  49 Plot the graph of $y = 37 - 5x$ on the grid above.

  50 What are the **coordinates** of the point where the two lines intersect? (_____, _____)

7

Paper 18

Calculate the following values.

1 0.48 as a fraction in its **lowest terms** _____

2 $\frac{5}{8}$ as a decimal _____

3 $85 \times 2.5 =$ _____

4 $207 \div 0.9 =$ _____

5 17^2 _____

6 6^3 _____

If $m = 1$, $n = 2$, $t = 3$, what are the values of these?

7 $mnt =$ ____   **8** $m + n - t =$ ____

9 $t^2 - m^2 - n^2 =$ ____   **10** $n^2mt =$ ____

11 $\dfrac{m + n}{t} =$ ____   **12** $\dfrac{nt}{m} =$ ____

How many minutes are in each of these?

13 $\frac{1}{2}$ a day _____ minutes

14 $\frac{2}{3}$ of an hour _____ minutes

15 $\frac{7}{12}$ of half an hour _____ minutes

A kilogram of tea costs x pounds and a kilogram of coffee costs y pounds.

16 What is the cost of 2 kilograms of tea and 3 kilograms of coffee? £ _____

17 What is the cost of a kilograms of tea and b kilograms of coffee? £ _____

Cube

Tetrahedron

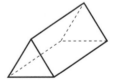
Triangular prism

18–23 Complete this table.

Name of shape	Number of faces	Number of vertices	Number of edges
Cube	6	8	____
Tetrahedron	4	____	____
Triangular prism	____	____	____

24 Using this table, write an equation relating **faces** (F) and **vertices** (V) to **edges** (E).

_____

25 What is the name of the shape shown on the grid below? _____

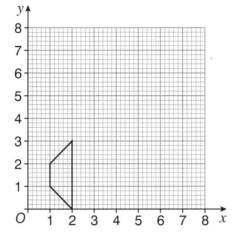

26 Given that each large square is 1cm², what is the area of the shape? _____

27–30 Enlarge the shape by a **scale factor** of 2 with (0, 0) as the centre of enlargement. What are the **coordinates** of the **vertices** of the enlarged shape?

(_____, _____) (_____, _____) (_____, _____) (_____, _____)

31 What is the area of the enlarged shape? _____

32 How many times greater is the enlarged area than the original area? ___

8

Continue these sequences.

B7/B10

33–34 1 $3\frac{1}{2}$ 6   ___   ___

35–36 25   5   1   ___   ___

37–38 16   18   24   34   ___   ___

6

39–44 Complete this table.

B 20

	Length (cm)	Breadth (cm)	Area (cm²)	Perimeter (cm)
Rectangle A	19.5	7	_____	_____
Rectangle B	16	_____	88	_____
Rectangle C	_____	11	_____	49

6

For any size of circle: Area = πr²

Take π to be 3.14.

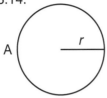

A

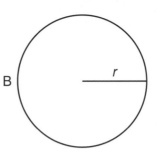

B

The area of circle A is 153.86 cm². The area of circle B is 379.94 cm².

45 What is the radius of circle A? ____

46 What is the radius of circle B? ____

47 Calculate the **mean** of these test scores.

   9   6   6   8   12   9   17   7   ____

48–49 The sum of two numbers is 82, and their difference is 26. What are
the two numbers? ____ and ____

50 If I travel 156 km in $2\frac{1}{2}$ hours, what is my average speed? ____ km/h

Now go to the Progress Chart to record your score! **Total** ⃝ **50**

Paper 19

Calculate the answers to these.

1 65.26 − 2.53 = _____   **2** 16.14 + 103.28 = _____

3 66.14 × 4 = _____   **4** 20.8 ÷ 0.8 = _____

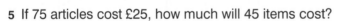

5 If 75 articles cost £25, how much will 45 items cost? £ _____

6 How many whole years are there in 9241 weeks? _____ years

7 Calculate the **mean** for this set of numbers.

   0.6   1.0   0.4   0.2   0.9   1.1   1.2   0.5   0.9   0.7   ____

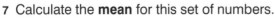

8 In a local store an item, priced at £110, is sold for £96.25.
What percentage discount is given? _____%

B2/B12
1

9 I think of a number, divide it by 4, and then add 5 to give an answer of 11.
What was the number I first thought of? _____

B2/B3

10 If 5 kg of cheese costs £42.50, how much will 1.5 kg cost? £ _____

B 3

11 What is the surface area of a cube whose **edge** is 15 cm long? _____ cm²

B20/B21
3

One number is chosen at random from 9, 10, 11, 12, 13, 14, 15, 16, 17 and 18. Writing your answers as fractions in the **lowest terms**, what is the probability of choosing:

B16/B10
B6/B5

12 a **square number**? _____

13 a **multiple** of 3? _____

14 a **prime number**? _____

15 a **multiple** of 2? _____

4

Calculate the answers to these.

B3/B6

16 $3 \times (-10) =$ _____

17 $(-5) \times (-6) =$ _____

18 $10 \div (-5) =$ _____

19 $(-36) \div (-9) =$ _____

20 $36 \div (-3)^2 =$ _____

5

21–26 Here are two nets for an open-topped box. Draw six different nets.

B 21

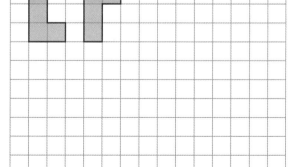

6

Simplify these expressions.

27 $x^2 - (x^2 - y^2) =$ _____

28 $(a - 2z) - (z - 2a) =$ _____

29 $1 + b - (1 - b) =$ _____

30 $2(c - d) - (c + d) =$ _____

31 $3(f + h) - 2(h - f) =$ _____

Calculate the answers to these fraction problems. Give answers in the **lowest terms**. Use **mixed numbers** where appropriate.

32 $\frac{3}{5} + \frac{2}{3} =$ _____

33 $\frac{5}{8} - \frac{1}{4} =$ _____

34 $1\frac{7}{8} - \frac{11}{16} =$ _____

35 $2\frac{1}{2} \times \frac{2}{3} \times \frac{1}{3} =$ _____

36 $6\frac{1}{4} \div 3\frac{1}{3} =$ _____

Calculate the length and breadth of each of these rectangles using the information given below.

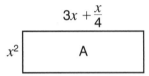

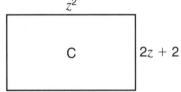

Perimeter = 21 cm   Area = 13.5 cm²   Perimeter = 74 cm

37–38 Rectangle A has a length of ____ cm and a breadth of ____ cm.

39–40 Rectangle B has a length of ____ cm and a breadth of ____ cm.

41–42 Rectangle C has a length of ____ cm and a breadth of ____ cm.

Now use the dimensions that you have determined to answer these.

43 A has an area of _____ cm².

44 B has a perimeter of _____ cm.

45 C has an area of _____ cm².

Solve these **simultaneous equations**.

46–47 $t + 2z = 12$ and $z = 4t$ $t =$ _____ $z =$ _____

48–49 $c = 3 - 2d$ and $d = 12 - 2c$ $c =$ _____ $d =$ _____

Pythagoras' theorem states that:

'In any right-angled triangle, the square of the hypotenuse (longest side) is equal to the sum of the squares of the other two sides.' Use this rule to calculate the size of the base of a right-angled triangle that has an hypotenuse of 50 cm and a perpendicular height of 30 cm.

50 Base = ____ cm

Paper 20

Calculate these percentages.

B 12

1 16% of £125   £ ___

2 $17\frac{1}{2}$ % of £350   £ ___

3 25% of £18   £ ___

4 18% of £1.50   ___ p   **4**

5–9 Put these in order from largest to smallest.   B6/B11   B 10   **5**

$$-0.349 \qquad -\frac{8}{27} \qquad -0.36 \qquad -\frac{1}{3} \qquad -0.35$$

___   ___   ___   ___   ___

10 Cilla has 6 DVDs, 18 CDs and 42 videos. What is the ratio of Cilla's DVDs to CDs to videos, in simplest form?   ___   B 13

11 If 35 sheep were sold at the local farm auction for £1647.50, what would 49 sheep have cost at the same rate?   £ ___   B 3

12 Simplify $\dfrac{12z^3}{4z^2}$.   ___   B8/B10   **3**

Calculate the answers to these.   B6/B2

13 $3^2 + 2^2 =$ ___   **14** $7^2 - 5^2 =$ ___   B 8

15 $2^3 + 3^2 =$ ___   **16** $(8^2 - 2^2) + 3^3 =$ ___   **4**

Calculate the answers to these.   B2/B8

17 $12 - (9 - (7 - 5)) =$ ___

18 $2(17 + 3) - (17 + (10 - 3)) + 3.4 =$ ___

19 $2(11 - 10) + 3(10 - 8) - 4(9 - 7) =$ ___

20 $(12 - 7) + (6 - 3) + 18 + 20 =$ ___   **4**

Express the numbers below as products of **prime factors**, using **indices** where you can.   B5/B6

21–22 $108 =$ ___ × ___   **23–24** $676 =$ ___ × ___   **25–26** $200 =$ ___ × ___   **6**

27 A game, priced at £8, is sold for £6.40. What percentage discount is given? ___ %   B2/B12

28 What is the total number of hours in the last six months of the year? ___ hours   B 27

29 Calculate the **mean** for this set of numbers.   B 15

  15.3   16.2   12.8   13.5   16.3   17.6   15.9   14.8   ___   **3**

Calculate the angles marked *a*, *b* and *c*.

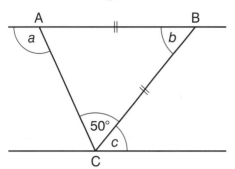

AB = BC

30 Angle *a* = _____ °   **31** Angle *b* = _____ °   **32** Angle *c* = _____ °

 5

Calculate the volume and surface area of each of these cuboids.

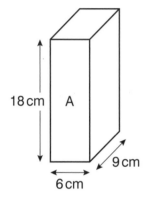

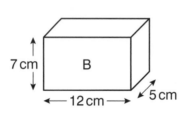

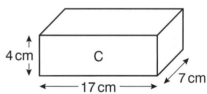

33 Cuboid A has a volume of _____

34 Cuboid A has a surface area of _____

35 Cuboid B has a volume of _____

36 Cuboid B has a surface area of _____

37 Cuboid C has a volume of _____

38 Cuboid C has a surface area of _____

39–40 The sum of two numbers is 25 and their difference is 3. What are the two numbers? _____ and _____

The perimeter of a rectangle is 30 cm, and its length is 3 cm more than its breadth.

    41 What is the length? _____

    42 What is the breadth? _____

    43 What is the area? _____

Calculate the answers to these fraction problems.

B 10

44 $2\frac{3}{4} + 3\frac{5}{8} =$ _____

45 $5\frac{2}{3} \times 3\frac{3}{4} =$ _____

46 $6\frac{3}{4} \div 2\frac{5}{8} =$ _____

47 $4\frac{1}{4} \times \frac{3}{5} \times \frac{2}{5} =$ _____

4

Solve these **simultaneous equations**.

B 8

$$x - 3y = -1 \qquad 2x - 4y = 2$$

48 $x =$ _____   **49** $y =$ _____

4

According to Pythagoras' theorem; the square of the hypotenuse (longest side) of any right-angled triangle, is equal to the sum of the squares of the other two sides. Use this rule to find the length of the hypotenuse of a right-angled triangle that has a base of 24 cm and a height of 32 cm.

B 18

50 Length = _____ cm

5

Now go to the Progress Chart to record your score!   Total   50

Progress Chart   Maths 12⁺–13⁺ years

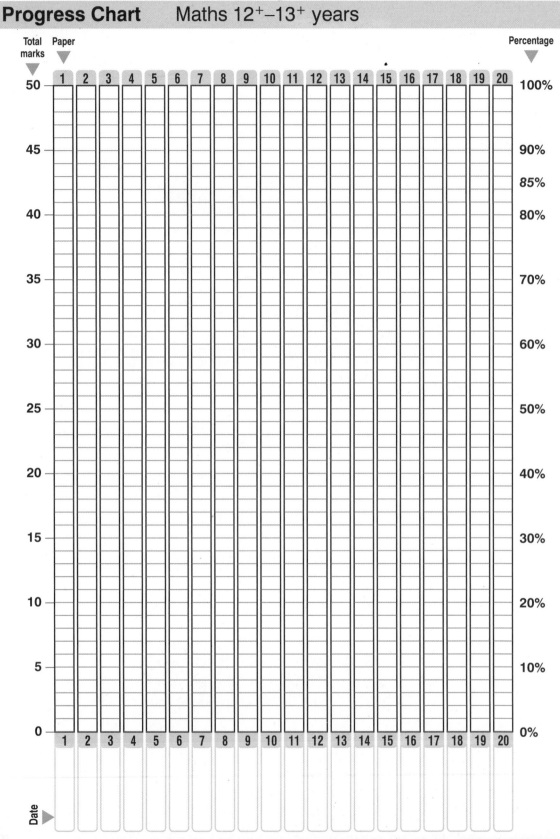

Total marks

Paper

Percentage

| 1 | 2 | 3 | 4 | 5 | 6 | 7 | 8 | 9 | 10 | 11 | 12 | 13 | 14 | 15 | 16 | 17 | 18 | 19 | 20 |

50 — 100%

45 — 90%
— 85%

40 — 80%

35 — 70%

30 — 60%

25 — 50%

20 — 40%

15 — 30%

10 — 20%

5 — 10%

0 — 0%

| 1 | 2 | 3 | 4 | 5 | 6 | 7 | 8 | 9 | 10 | 11 | 12 | 13 | 14 | 15 | 16 | 17 | 18 | 19 | 20 |

Date

When you've finished the book use the Next Steps Planner